T0345232

The
China
Sketchbook

THE INDIA LIST

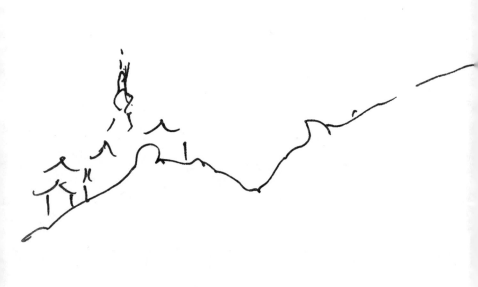

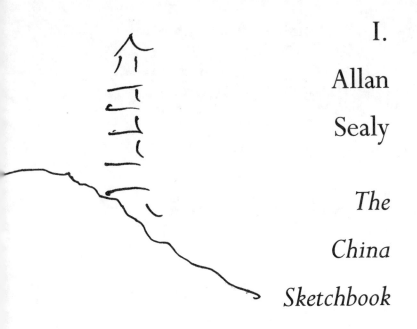

I.
Allan
Sealy

The
China
Sketchbook

LONDON NEW YORK CALCUTTA

Seagull Books, 2016

Text and images © I. Allan Sealy, 2016
This compilation © Seagull Books, 2016

First published by Seagull Books in 2016

ISBN 978 0 8574 2 397 9

British Library Cataloguing-in-Publication Data
A catalogue record for this book is available
from the British Library

Designed by Sunandini Banerjee, Seagull Books, Calcutta, India
Printed and bound by Hyam Enterprises, Calcutta, India

Contents

Balsam poplar

(into the airport road)

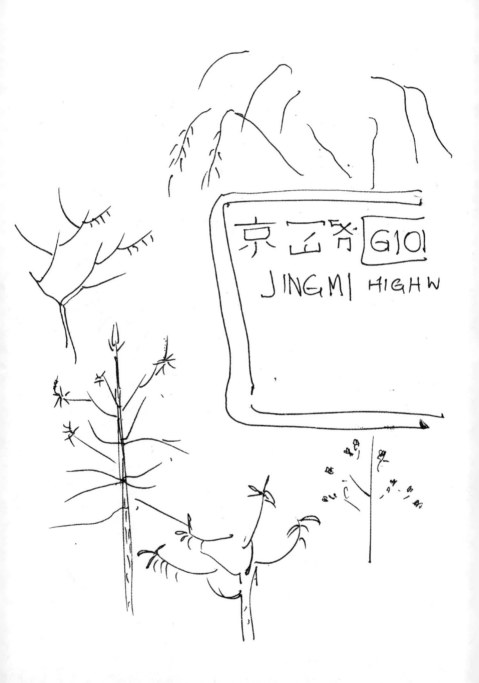

cellphone tower and deodar

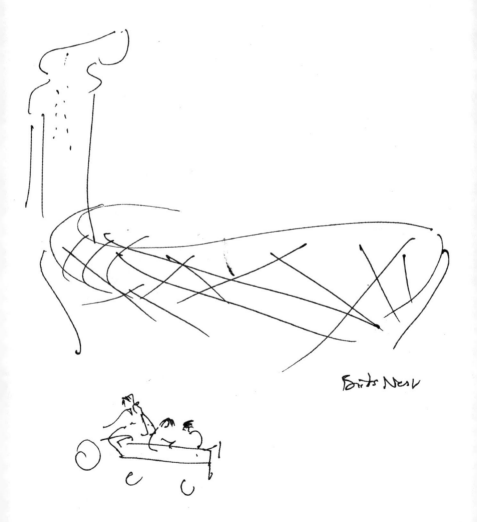

印度 (India)

茶 tea

21 Men   noofp 310

Dreams close to the
surface : तातनी 21 says
one woman young as always
Duvets , no blankets, so
top cold bottom hot. Packed
like a movie : five pants
two shirts , no art pen —
slipped away

I live at the hotel
today : checkout is
every 24 hrs. All
young women look
my age , all young
men puppies

cement inlay tile
outside 310

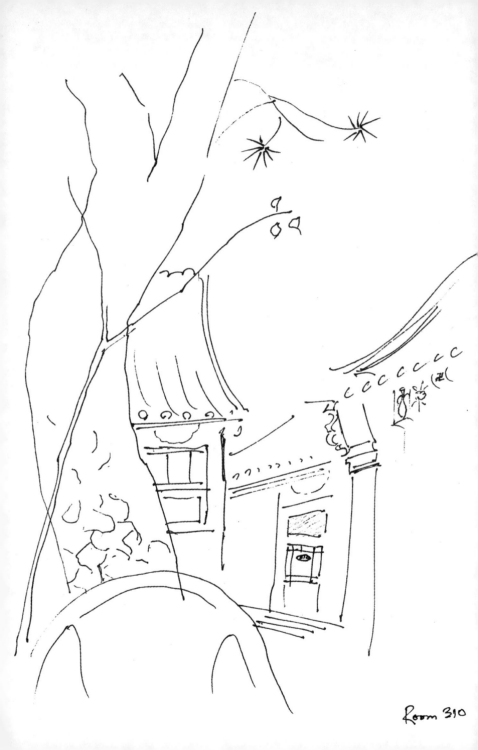

Room 310

deer

rabbit

香山
fragrant hill

bulldozed path to
clearing

Quan Ju De

Li Xiang Ting, Mr

李祥霆 先生

演奏 plays

古 琴 lute
vino
Gu Qin

（唐代古琴，1300年前）

the oldest musical score in existence

Tang Dynasty 755 CE

Li Yanhua 李艳华
yaliya @ yahoo.com

Sophora japonica everywhere   (the city tree of Xi'an)
Ancient cypress avenue to Wofosi   – city flower: pomegranate
in tubs at the Sunday market
Catalpa bungei 800 年 at Small Pagoda
Pomegranate in blossom outside the city wall Xi'an
Paulownia leaf picked through a crenellation!
Cherries in season, 50¥ a kilo : the seller spoke good
Lichis not as good as the rose-scented at D-101   young man
Jackfruit ripe flakes separated (gloves) and sold by the p
Dried fruit of every kind – dates, figs even kiwi (Chinese
Walnuts forming in the treetops   gooseberry after all
Ginkgo groves and walks in gardens and streets
Purple oxalis, pale pink flower, a pot plant
Masses of petunia, marigold in parterre
Cactus in a windowbox is someone's garden
House-high trees transplanted by the truckload
Instant forest at Cloud Ridge Caves
Roses thrive on Beijing highway divide
Lovers disappear into nightwood by highway
Almonds forming at Wofo gardens
Willow by tombstone in trackside graveyard

Iris bed in
Magnolia Garden

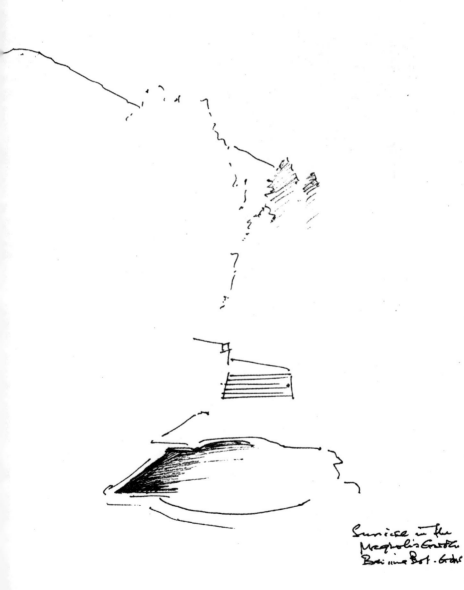

Sunrise in the
Magnolia Grotto
Beijing Bot. Gdns

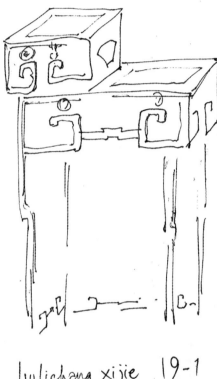

CONVENIEN
HOTEL

liulichang xijie 19-1

ji = ~~apostrophe~~
min Zao Xu ti

chinatravelguide.com

ctrip.com
chinatour.net

Lao Xu di Restaurant
Beijing Belly Day
Sunday 23 May

MAO
LIVEHOUSE
ROCK LIVE & BAR
门 了 大 地 一 门 号

Gong & Drum Hutong
nan luo gu xian

Minor Nationalities Park

UNIVERSITY	大学	da xue
ROOM	房间	fang jian
LOW PRICE	低价	di jia
BANK	银行	yin hang
ATM	自动取款机	zi dong qu kuan ji
TOILET	洗手间	xi shou jian
WATER	水	shui
TRAIN	火车	huo che
BUS	汽车	qi che
STATION	车站	che zhan
AIR PORT	机场	ji chang

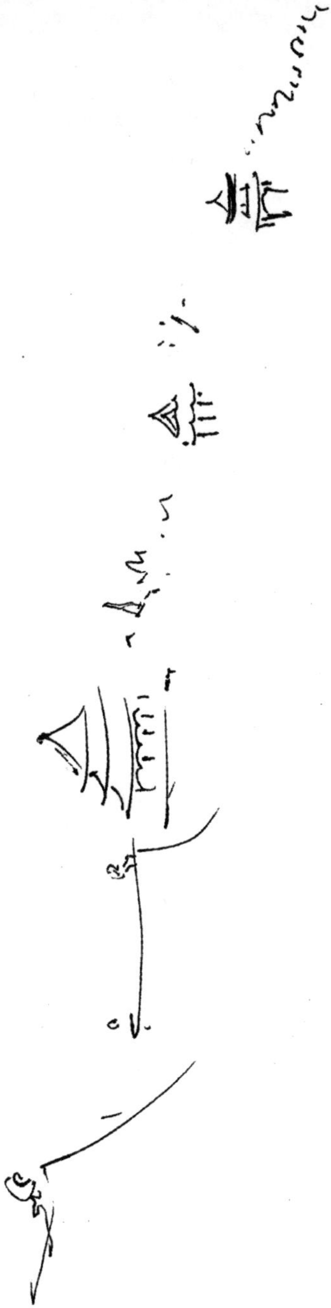

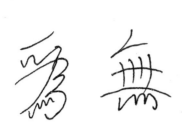

槐树
"huai" tree

Scholar tree
from which the last Ming hanged himself

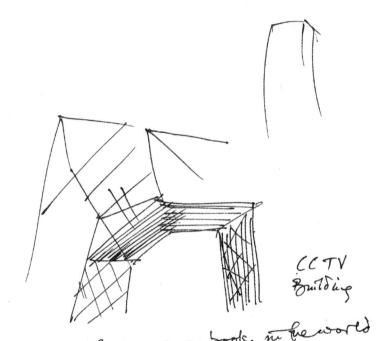

CCTV
Building

VN (But every city of r every book in the world
look like (pointing over his shoulder)
AN what do you have against nostalgia? It's a
poor man's sociology
IAS (thinks) sociology is a rich man's nostalgia..
I have now seen [correcting last night's structure]
a good Beijing building.
LL (eyes shining)
LT (nods, smiles)
then we pass the burnt out shell of the other
CCTV building and Vivek exults!

Rem Koolhas · 库哈斯

西川
Xi Chuan

Gefei

Zhai Yongming

Chinese currency notes stink like ours.
No dust in China. Towel rail in free black wood
Dove is always forward phlegmy
Dogs never nobody's, except once.
No cockroaches in China. One fly and two
                                        mosquitoes.
Street calls here too
No one stares but all take a second look at the In-
Sparrows browner than ours, swallows blacker

Fethi in Balwiddin's room
25 May 2010

dinze
golden pond

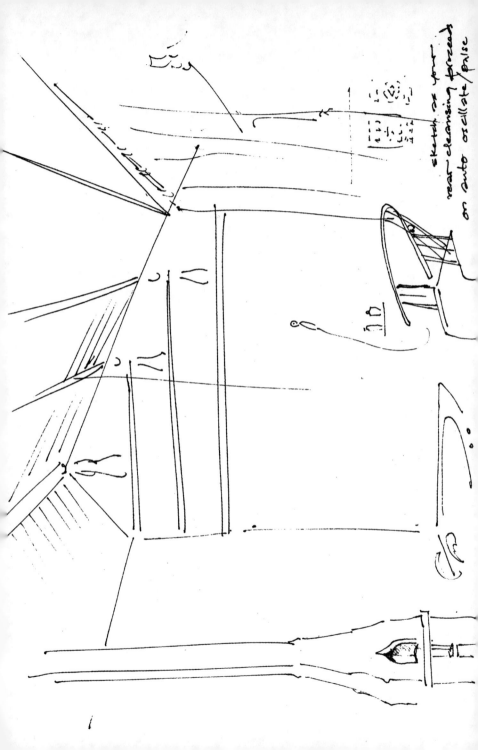

sketch as you
wear cleansing forward
on auto oscillate/pulse

Teahouse

Mr Hu architect and painter, builder of this reconstructed mews would have liked to have visited India sooner to have incorporated its elements in his work

Mr Zhang millionaire and patron. says people feel poor not because they have no money but because they have no control over their lives. We are building this traditional quarter as a lamentation because China is no longer China

Mr Hu : Land cannot be sold so peasants are poor but when it can where will they be?

Mr Lucie-Smith: In the West Indies where I come from (Jamaica) for example in Haiti : land was split up and overworked. Haiti has had the topsoil stripped off and that is why it is poor : fly over the border and you see the difference on the Dom. Rep. side.

Rukmini : The difference is due to France's repatriation of Haitian wealth ... Peasants can carry their skills when they sell

Kabir : Contentment with the self .. Ghatak evinces neither a desire to go back nor an anxiety to say something new. Ray makes a clear break. follows the French. Ghatak is a door to lost alleys, a river, a depth. Depth, of which there is little in the Chinese new wave of the 80s, is an eternal value

A good artist must lament politically, be a go

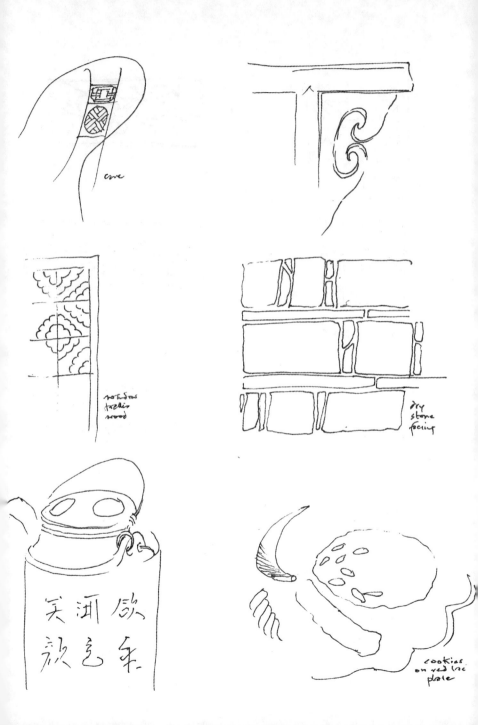

cave

window
trellis
wood

dry
stone
facing

欲河欲
歌乌未

cookies
on red lac
plate

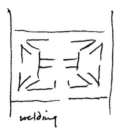

welding

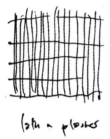

lath n plaster

pollarded pome
granote

top rail of
towel horse

file fascia

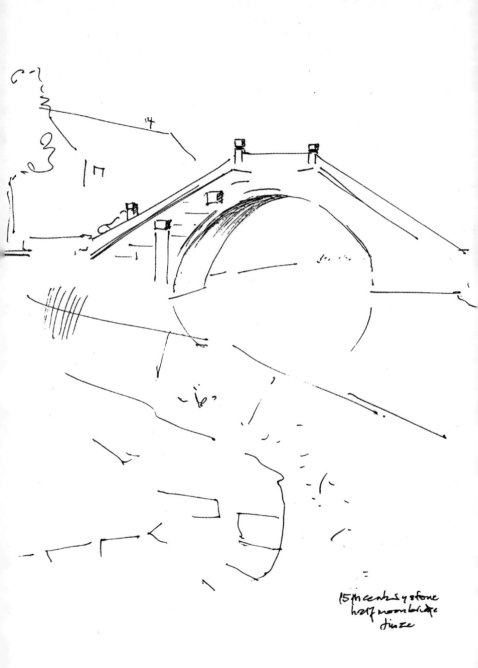

15th century stone
half moon bridge
Suzhou

Zhujiajiao. canal town with 33 bridges on the Yangtze delta. Old lady in wheel-
chair asked to be turned around to watch the poetry of ludos

Things I didn't ~~buy~~:

The yellow ~~jackfruit~~ segments ~~peeled~~ with her gloved fingers
The blue glazed pottery jardinière at the Sunday market
Loquats; was I late?
Great fat wrinkled dates, Hui or Mongol
A bushy paintbrush ~~for~~ washes. An inkstone
Green tea. Jasmine tea.
The silver necklace, 25 π, with a spiral on the medal
Walnut butter freshly ground, a jar
A canary, caged, among harassed birds
A handsome yellow suit of clothes for a three-year-old, red
Blown glass blue with white spirals from a roadside tab
Flat noodles in a single portion crockpot casserol
A golden labrador on a leash, sitting good-naturedly
A hollow wooden croaking frog, serrated, with strok
City maps from old women
Biscuits to munch on with the Nescafé 2ml sachets
Soft leather? imitation leather moccasins
A Dicos chicken drumstick
A black and white and red mask at the airport shop
Maoist memorabilia

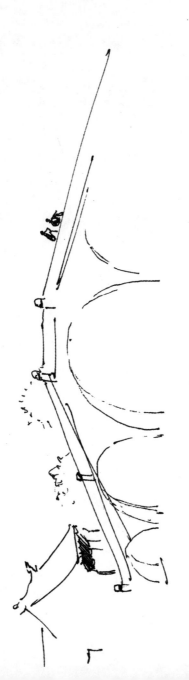

Zhujiajian

→ Dinner by the river after boatride (collision noted as to the wheel boat)
Muddy river fish, whole cluster soup, *shooting potatoes, rices/greens, roasted, *eggplant soft purple
Shunplayer and other performed on x etc

Er hu 胡月

① 天涯歌女　　Wandering Sing song girl

② 黄梅戏　　Huang Mai opera

③ 好一朵茉莉花　　What a beautiful magnolia

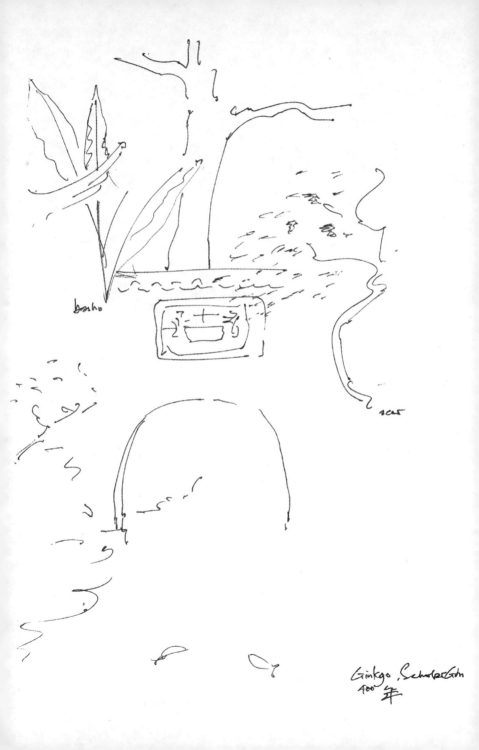

basho

acer

Ginkgo ScholarGrtn
400 年

Charcoal grey ceiling, white walls : Akurah restaura

Charcoal grey tile dado, white walls : Zhangs bathroo

Grilled salmon
· perfection

空
糸工
羅

AKURAH 2   Japanese restaurant & bar

Shanghai University dinner

frogs legs deep fried
bok choy
beef w tomato (summering)
chicken w chestnuts
chicken feet with small sharp pepper
spring rolls fresh filled
prawns with yellow bean
broad beans
roast beef (sliced cold)
marinated radish (yellow brown)
squid w gr pepper (long sweet)
steamed river fish Yangzi
fish head soup
green beans
Hunan fish tails (Mao's with red chili)

plain rice
congee w fruit apple/pineapple
dates in sauce
seaweed
watermelon sliced & seeded

sorghum biryani (Xian)
beef soup and flatbread (Xian)
stirfried chicken with red bell peppers (Pingyao)
grilled skewered lamb (Huohota)
steamed dumplings (Datong)
egg drop soup (for eight!) (Huohota, Malaqi fandian)
Mountain mushrooms & celery soup (Pingyao)
                          & seaweed
roast pork & pickled eggs (Jinze)
steamed whole riverfish (Zhujiajiao)

my upstairs room
at Juza

Shanghai University

Ashoth : Cochin — every culture depends on the other for its view of itself. Such tolerance is more attainable than the enlightenment type which requires the shedding of all prejudice. The 1992 anthropologized census shows 15% of the population have more than one religion. In the 1947 genocide: 40% of respondents say they were helped by the other community and owe their survival to members of that group.

Vivek : Realism has become a default mode through fear of subjectivity and _Almost Island_ is an attempt to change that

Angry Young Woman : Subjectivity can turn extreme and neglect reality.

Novelist : I would like to ask the fiction writers where they stand ...

IAS : I have just turned away from fiction in my present book, but at one point I changed a man's real name control + F = 26 changes instantly, but also: _instant fic_

Angry Young Woman : The point was not the permeability of fiction and non-fiction but an acknowledgement that fiction has failed to address certain realities.

Professor [not angry, not young, not a woman, debonair expensively dressed unlike the other academics in the room, designer olive jacket, belt tie shoes]: we cannot neglect our social responsibility; literature may have gone too far in the opposite direction.

Angry Young Woman : _dintian's day_ may have passed and with it Bei Dao's.

Beijing 29 May

Sat evening: Dongchan Gongyuan blocked off
by freq. lowering goose-stepping squad; got off at
Tianmanmen East instead of West and missed the garden
So it waiting for 8pm. Train to Xian ab 9·30. Metro
to Military Museum then taxi to Beijing West Stn.
    7·50 lights come on! The whole shebang flood'it
just as I was about to leave ... gold, green, maroon
jewel box. Saturday night crowd milling against the
dusk. Sun went down just over the forbidden park!

Xian   30 May

Hammers tee on the young woman on the other upper
berth in the soft sleeper coupe to Xian. Took the Metro
from Tiananmen to Military Museum stop, then walked
to Beijing West Stn exulting: my first freedom in ten
days, freedom of the city of the country. A woman cries
as her lover hugs her goodbye on the platform and my
heart goes out to her.

Woke at 5 in the mountains: cave dwellings,
Christian cemeteries .. then rest till arrival at 8.30. Walk
straight through the touts   breakfast at McDonald's
(after foul WC, first Indian toilet of the journey. By stat
then bus 611 to Muslim Qtr. bus woman driver helpful
(asking my way all along pointing at the Chinese in the:
Chance on the Youyi Hotel and rejoice.

Clean linen, double bed, hot shower (three today
each time I come home) Reharganj plus bathroom &
Sunday market full of canaries and kittens, a golden
labrador more beautiful than the illuminated Drum To
than the blonde dolly birds, than the Princess Yong Tai ..
figs, mushrooms, huge cooked livers I thought were
turtles, cherries, dates, pigs feet, jade, mock silver
horn combs, rush slippers ..

Lunch a bowl of yangrou paomo with a flat biscuit
like bread broken into the beef soup. Garnished at the
table (shredded first) with coriander & green onions, and
served with a sweetish pickled garlic which the cook
showed me how to peel.   Dinner two lamb skewers
with a pizza sized naan : 45¥ the hard faced woman
with the head-scarf many were punched on the calculat
while the nice young waiter clenched his smile as he
saw I was being cheated. Wanted to floss her right out
of my mouth but brushed vigorously thinking you
lose some ..

Helpful boy at the Info Centre gave me a map

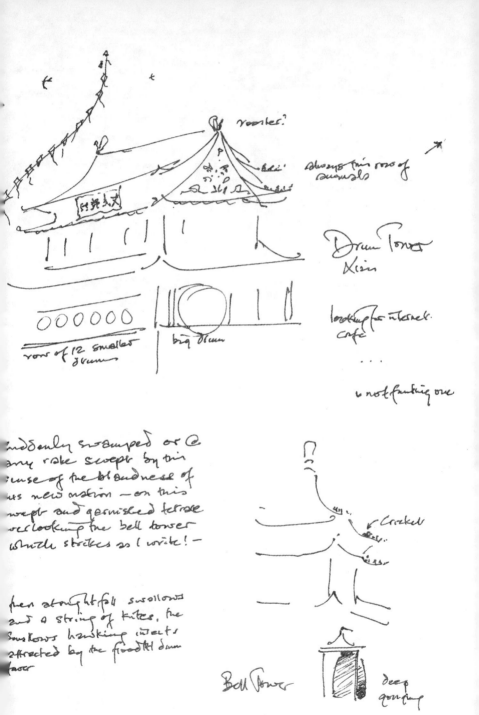

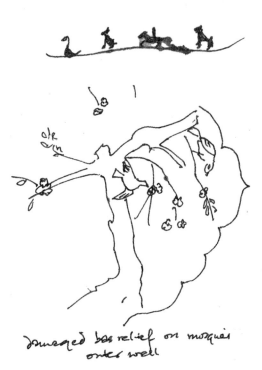

Damaged bas relief on mosque's
outer well

Chance on the net
while looking for an
net cafe

Afterwards find it
my street! Youyi
stone end of a sou
with old doorways o
opposite the mosque
Behind the mosque
bakery selling yesterd
discus too hot to hand
(straight off the stan
tabletop-sized griddl
Smiling concierge gi
me a fresh flask of h
water for Nescafe so

Munir the benefactor must be home by now : set out
his Silk route the day we left for Shanghai

Ancient stone block
on the paved approach
to the Small Wild Goose
Pagoda (Monk Du Shun's)
in Sifu Village Changan
Dist Dharma Master Du
Shun 557-640 AD

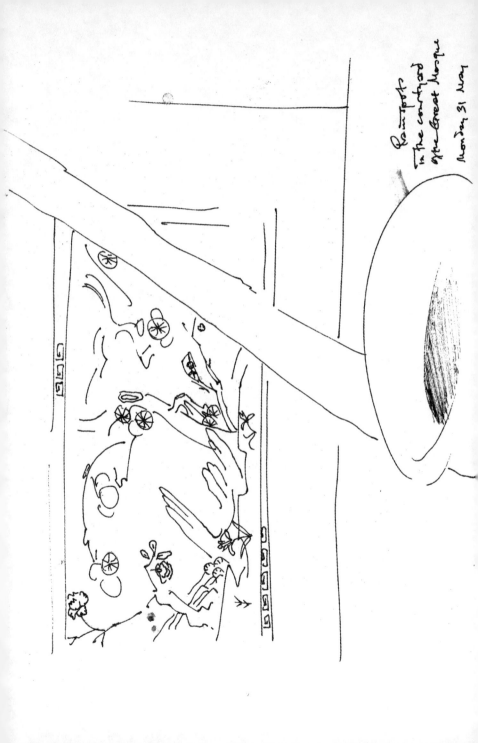

Rooftops
in the courtyard
of the Great Mosque

Monday 31 May

Painted pottery
Tang 618-90?

Pedestal with engraved
musicians
Tang Dynasty
618-907

Stone Slab of
Shijun's To

Northern Zhou
557–81

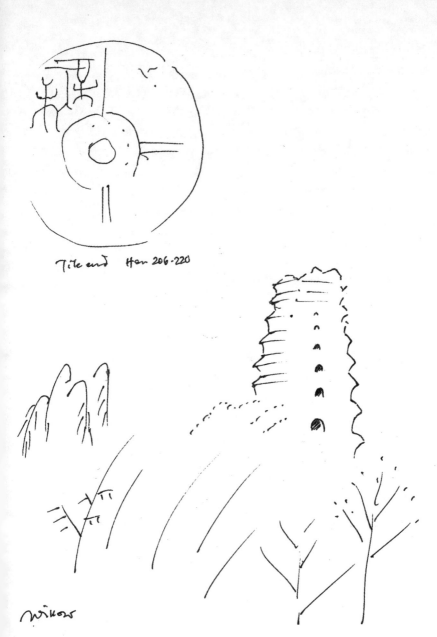

Tile end   Han 206-220

willows

Bamboo   Poplars   Ginkgo

Small Wild Goose
Pagoda

31 May

Chinese cybercafes are steeped in darkness so you must be a touch typist or perish. Today a Chang-an joy: even stumbled on the Xi'an museum while in the heavenly garden of the lesser goose. Pottery to gladden the heart while the rain dripped outside. Afterwards bussed to the greater goose but needn't have bothered the Dharma Master "Rabbi" Xuan Zang was present in a 16thc ink drawing by 井井 万历 年间. But fine recreation of Chang-an in the museum and a gentle mist descending through the deodars in the temple of Hsuen's brother made the day. 8th century (or 800 year) catalpas among the ancient trees. Have got quite used to Xi'an city buses jumping on and off for a single like a local, yet to take a taxi.

Dinner an appetiser of grilled lamb at one stall then a whole steamed fish, extraordinary, with rice 10¥ for the fish & rice so last night's 45¥ for two sticks of lamb & one tandoori roti was robbery. Tonight's was gentle, sweet-faced, last night's a headscarfed gorgon

Rain dousing my terracotta warrior plans: leave it till the afternoon of the train? Want to get a sleeper the Yulin K train, 12 hrs, leaving at 10 pm. Then either Hohot & Datong or D and H depending on links. Yulin because it's a border outpost on the Great Wall the sort of place no one would want to go to.

Women bus drivers — and they're all women — ever helpful, patient, watchful (that last look in the mirror) inventive with signs; "cross the street and catch the bus going the other way!" spoken with the hands. Sign language brings you right up against the person: words get in the way.

明 万历年间
1573 - 1620

June 1

Woke to rooster crowing. Drizzling all night from the sound of the overflow. In amongst the street cries yesterday thought I heard the house telephone and stiffened – thousands of miles away. A whole Xuan Zang journey, free of those cares, no dreaded gatelatch.

But the rain washes out the terracotta warriors: tomorrow afternoon then, after checkout and left luggage. Shirt washed and drying, now book Yulin train, buy phonecard to contact the Chinese tell them I'm OK. OK the one word every Chinese knows. Eating cold dry bread helped down with warm Nescafe, bless Junir's heart. Today finish the browning lichis, tomorrow a fresh start. This hotel has been a haven, feel comfortable, clean, restored, and every time I come back, secure.

Making a missing buttonhole in the black shirt with nailclippers necessary because in trial run the whole roller of dollars slipped out and fell softly to the ground – Jesus Jesus Jesus – so black threads scattered around me like nail parings in this bed

4.30 Ticket to Pingyao in hand, bicycle parked aside me on the wall, the city wall of Xi'an!

moat

walnut tree fruiting

avenue of ginkgos

pomegranate   pomegranate

northwest corner of
Xian city wall
with bend in moat

5.10pm

Bizzyle weather as 24 hrs of drizzle
lets up. Cool misty mild. Walk along
the south face (pomegranate in flower
all along) looking for a way up
to the top — no idea I'd find bicycles
on the wall..

q the west wall

might have hesitated
if I'd known the length
of the wall : 13.7 km
But such exhileration
setting out! The east
wall hesnous hill then
down hill on the home
stretch to the south
gate. Long stretches
with no one in sight:
once a lone cleaner
dusting off a bronze
bin. As I finished the
dustbin sketch a woman
and her mother and aunt
(two grey heads anyway)
stopped to watch and
then gave me the same thumbs
up sign the erhu player
gave me. Tried to converse
but they repeated good
and beautiful ; we smiled
and nodded for a minute.
Later three women of my
age, disoriented, asked
me a question in Chinese
Each face of the wall has
its own symbol on grapple
and bin lid. Looked down
from the north wall on the
scene of this morning's
debacle : Xi'an Station
where I stood in a queue
(line jumper eased in ahead
of me, another ahead of the
woman behind — to a scolding)
only to be told : no train ..

Dustbin on NW corner

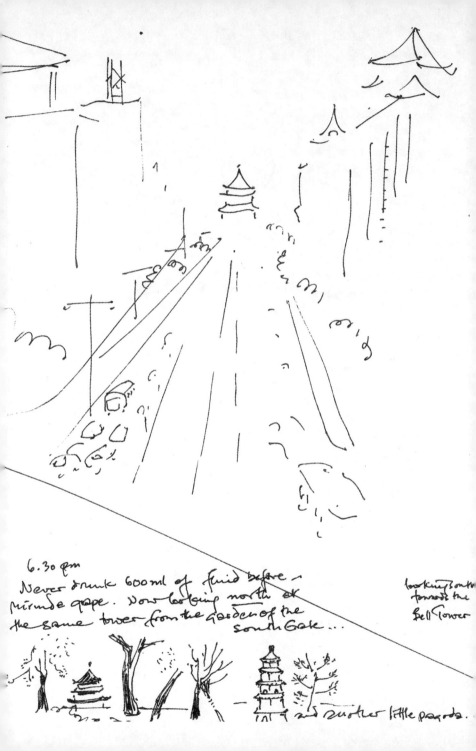

6.30 pm
Never drunk 600ml of fluid before ~
Mirinda grape. Now looking north at
the Game tower from the garden of the
South Gate ...

looking south
toward the
Bell Tower

~ and another little pagoda.

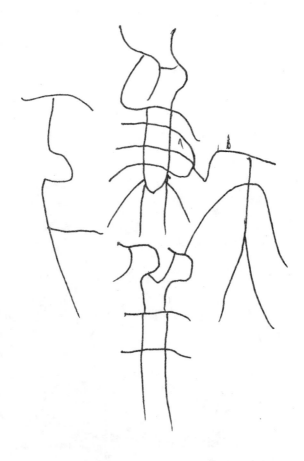

Li Si's 4 character poem

oldest wall
in China

cinnamon grass!

Cappucino after sonsciove: treasure such
moments of utter solitude,
vistas of empty landscaping.

Whatcan those crowded alleys, those packed dwellings do
to the spirit? Brushing, even knocking a stranger is
nothing, no apology tendered or expected. Breakfast
restauranteur said something civil as I left but w
the trace of a smile, and yet the hotel lady exchanged
many nods and smiles as I checked out. Bowed,
offered my 60¥ change (20¥ kept back each day on
100¥) with both hands. Stood there holding her smile
I turned and shouldered my pack; when I turned at
door her beautiful smile still there and we exchanged
a last nod. Surly waitress not now, barely out of
teenage. Closing time, 5 pm, she furls each of the
umbrellas at the other tables. The last of the hordes
leaving; must now turn my face away from this lil
culdesac, find a bus back to Xi'an. Train at 9.16.

Yellow caps leaving: a distinctly working class group. There goes the droll drunk of the group surged... ...side with his stomach exposed. An army of service ...k too, mostly girls, in the eateries: welcome ...ubway! they chorus. Bus driver on green railway ...s here broke every driving rule, sneaking in where ...can't elbow, once pretending to use the petrol stn ...d rolling out the other side to skip a red light, ...pping on the freeway, blaring his horn.

a sort of style firing
then firecrackers
below

...ussoorie high hills to the east, the hills we crossed ...enter the Xi'an valley. The remains here overclad with ...asonry, like much of modern Xi'an, like every monument ...cept the little T... Xuan's Z Great Pagoda grossly overdressed.

Now sitting on the unkempt grass, sandals off, facing the parkland, back against the edge of an unrounded granite slab. Rounding needed on everything (ours goes to the other extreme). But this was the day I waited for, clear and cool, through those two rainy days with spattered pant-cuffs and muddy feet.

An hour on my back in the grass. A simple plinth one foot high can screen you from an army — something to be said for this monumental terrace (but it must be 50m wide so the crowd, even split off, don't find the edge). Sunlight finds my face through the pine needles picked out against the sky, it lights up the dance of midges, white against the green, black against the blue. Incessant voices to one side, strange birdcalls to the other. Why so few insects? The odd ant, no mosquitoes. Bright green perfectly dry dark green pines, also the pawlonia like leaf on a tall slender sal-like tree: labelled, its a disc catching the sunlight so I cd check if I wanted. The empty windows of the exhibition hall look down at me; all else is green. Behind me all grey stone and pale cream skin, black hair, shocking pinks. A janitor empties the bin beside me — ni hao — he trundles his cart away. A peaceful ninety minute rest.

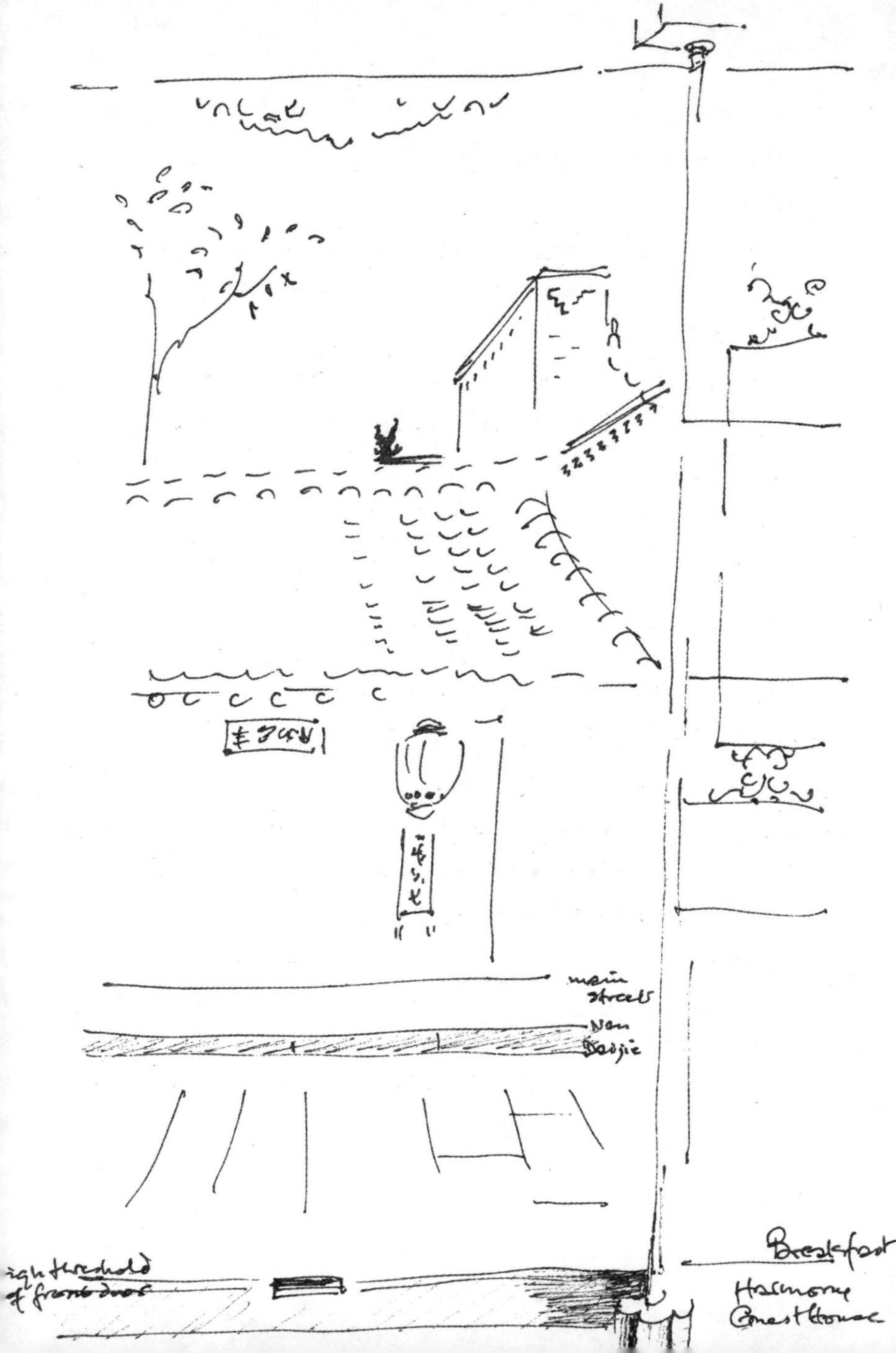

main
street

Nan
Godjie

Breakfast

Harmony
Guesthouse

right threshold
of front door

June 3

Pingyao. Sitting in the park outside the city wall. If this is the East Gate that's the roof of the Taoist temple to the right.

Arrived at 6 this morning, woken up by the woman cabin attendant as we rolled into the station: stuffed clothes and water into the pack and ran. Looking for a loo when c came up with a brochure showing Harmony Guest House a rate Single 80-100¥ So jumped in the back of his motor rickshaw and whizzed through a town not waking up. main street. Stopped outside a plain old door. Met Mr C who showed me first a 150¥ double then a 120¥ single. Sa pay 100 and he immediately agreed. Double bed occupies the whole of one end of the room, small clean bathroom with hot water. Washed clothes, showered, at breakfast tabl an Indian Canadian girl travelling for 2 months in Ch had done the works. Free internet, then ran to the loo. Next rented a bike — after arranging for Datong hard s and now riding through a truly unreconstructed town, th main street knickknacks actually not an excrescence c'd scrape away. Alley after alley of lived in courtyards.

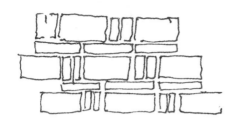

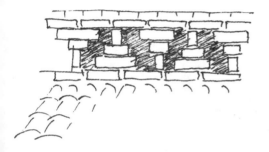

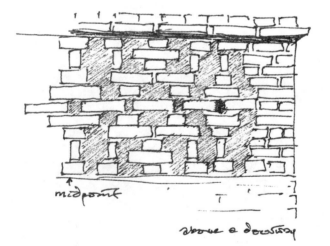

midpoint

above a doorway

李佩林 Eileen

菜侨 Maggie.

石姣 Shi Jiao

王珅 zoe

from Wuhan 武汉

fountain
Confucius ten
Peng 1980

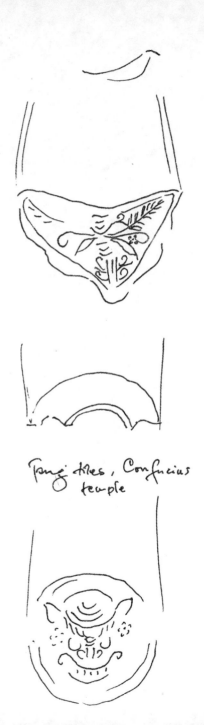

Pang tiles, Confucius
temple

Daoist scenes of torture and vengeance in hell while the good look on from the clouds: every kind of violence graphically rendered after the manner of Bosch

But the land god a smiling grey bearded old mandarin

It's a saying in Daoist that the person who does good things in his life will get a human being metempsychosis. The Metempsychosis Aunt sent the metempsychosis brother to give a baby who was the pre-existence person to every family

Zhangkui, Daoist god catching ghosts & demons

Robert Capa

罗伯特．卡帕

1913 - 1954   Italy, China

bear witness
I love you, Dad   1945
exhibition of photos

人陽曲鄭尉華

迷普

Ji Pu

永红

Yong Hong

(forever red
// forever bright)

Land God
Jade girl and G
Shuanglin Temple

唐槐

Tang Dynasty Scholar Tree

disheveled myself
the mirror of Lei Latais
est son. He had the
+ Room, lower down
in his father

After the Shaolin title straight home with the crippled motorcycle rickshawoman (she asked for 50¥ then came down to 30¥; I wrote down 25¥ and put a circle round it) [group from Xinjian come over to look, then a mother and daughter:

彭芃 → PENG PEING

China → shenzhe

who took a photo (of daughter and me) then more photos of these sketches, the last few pages] found myself on the street of Hei Luta grand residence on the very corner where I bega to think myself taken for a ride by the Harmony bro

The Hohot train is coming in, the whole plat quakes, and the girl in railway blue beside me i standing at attention looking straight into the en headlight protesting sweetly in my ear — the on two other passengers for train 1676 a man and w of my age are standing well back — "my English very poor!" She's racing against time would like keep me there and do her job; I'd like to keep h here and get to Hohot. Her arms are pressed a her side, hands open, fingers pointing straight dow the trouser seam the way all uniformed men an women stand on duty here and I say no your English is very good. No, she shouts, her voice brea yes! yes! I call back across the inches that divide

this pattern
in the wide
Si hotel

Lei Lidzis rooms
at the very back : summer tahkhana
on the local cave principle tucked under the
stair

6 am 5 June

Housed and fed, housed and fed. looking down
at trackside dwellings
chimneys up here, and
slate! blocks of black stone
A shutter! No: he's sitting
here playing his horn! Asses, the first birches,
weatherboard shacks flying the red flag. Ruined
villages, brick and clay, some dug out of the hillside.
Machine tilled fields, a lone hoer. Tiled brick
houses with yards, now hills

willows line a river, more asses, a led cow;
daubed clay washes away. Birches cut in half
sprouting at eight feet, poplar saplings in a double
row, alongside a single row of some conifer, then
a third row of some white flowering bush. A lake
with ducks, Hoopoe? Sheep! Lambs. The white
shine between the furrows plastic, not water; drifts
of it everywhere as it breaks down

Tibet Spring water "bottled at source". The train pulls smoothly out of a four-barrelled town: the woman beside me speaks to none with the same familiarity I would use for Haridwar or Roorkee. Her son eats noodles from a tub well sprung but badly buffered carriages.

duncecaps blue and red on a truly atrocious church

Spitting happens without the slightest preparation: pip! The young men this morning — not her son after all — smoking ceaselessly while I waited for the toilet. the railwayman at attention with his red & green flags

12 noon

Regency Hotel 100¥ for an airconditioned $50 room plateglassed-off bathroom out of some magazine. Dashed across the road like a local — everyone jaywalks — to check on the planner looking Railway Hotel : 200¥ — no: 219¥ so dashed back! Now sachet coffee and Xian muslim bread, the last cake showered and clothes washed and hung out, ready to hit this town.

Lesson still unlearnt :
the pursuit of depth — every added line diminishes the sketch
LEARN FOR THE ALMANAC

3pm Walked into the ground : what a wilderness
we have created, a machine gone crazy. I think
then see a patch of green that turns out to be central
park Hohot and duck into it. Find this cassia-like
tree (sophora japonica?) and drop into the grass under it
A boating pond but dreary,
the very greenery Indian
dusty. Still, a quiet spot
(industrial cutter starts up)
where no one bothers to
look.

The Malvagin waitress
warned me it was a big
bowl, only she was speaking
Chinese. Egg drop soup for
8 and three v. nice fresh
veg filled buns baked not
steamed. Ate one-eighth   malls malls mall
of the enormous bowl and was
pleased to see other bowls from crowded tables disappearing
behind a curtain where the staff appeared to be gathering
so hopefully the question thats tormented me all through
this journey is answered. At mere 27¥ the bill, compared
to the Muslim woman charges 45¥ for two skewers of la
and one 1¥ loaf of flatbread where no one but her prosper

Called Shenang from a PCO and when the man wro
9 raised my eyebrows and produced a 20¥ note. No, u
the girl said taking 2 1¥ note from my wallet : 9 tenths
of a yuan! Then I buy a filled jammy biscuit and a nar
                                    Khatai for — the b
Leave my tree where a   writes it down for b
human turd sent an   rather — 1.3 yuan /
occasional whiff across   I start to get the hang
the grass and find another of it : the tenths do
with softer greener grass   count for something
and — scented blossom   with small purchase
raining down on me : the
whole grove flowering!

Lilac bushes the flowers gone the green seed forming or I'd take some back to try. Man and his son come by picking dandelions and dropping them in a bag : salad, not weed.

Some kind of laburnum this, sweetly scented though so not our cassia : the flower cream not yellow. How she wanted to say more, the railway girl, and the language kept thwarting her. "Lower : you have lower" then I mimed which? high middle low. "Twelve is the carriage [carriage in Mandarin] eleven is the berth [berth in Mandarin] It will stop here [here in English]. It stopped a few feet ahead, to her great discomfiture and she apologized for the twelve paces I had to take. Then she had to hand me over to another blue girl and someone else accosted her appearing out of nowhere. The woman of my age was solicitous too pointing down the carriage towards 11. Men all say a little aloof. I like China I said and did it come out as I love China? She was overcome and flushed "Good. I know. Welcome to Pingyao!" As I was leaving.

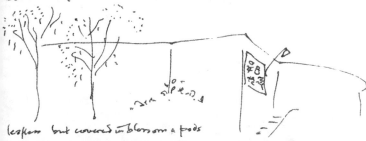

lespdeza but covered in blossom & pods

Sweet how in the green beside what turns out to be a dance academy little girls in lavender body suits & black tights and a piano thumping out Western tunes.

Sparrows in the trees, a tree pie long black tail walks through the long grass looking for something. Almost lost the cap of this pen by the other tree. Lay an hour and more with a handkerchief over my eyes and flowers raining down on nose and lips and folding in the wine with grass by my ear

_____

one falls as I write this on the page! With my face covered I could pass for a snoozing Mongol (layabout?) but the great marvel is this ground is covered in snow half the year round. Honey on the breeze threaded through by that single skein from the turd beyond the lilac bush by the other tree. Now go looking for the mosque only place to find a Mongol in this city.

6 June Didn't find the mosque but found the mongols in the Muslim quarter where every tall building is got up like a mosque and all the apartments are green and headscarves reappear and bakeries selling Mongol bread of which I bought three kinds, a plaited sugary baba an oversweet doughnut covered in sessame seeds, a domed quince bread cake, and a third I've yet to try. Also a peach as big as my fist eaten naked in the a/c room dripping all over. Called thus to say goodbye because there were phones where I stopped for water. Shops and restaurants a repeat of the mosque area in Xi'an.

DAO
LU

JINNA HOTEL

59

JINNA POST

angot quarter
shwe

In the ornate lobby of the Regency waiting for my train to Datong. Mongol kitsch or Mongol taste:

things could be much worse: ticket in hand
after a walk to the station leaving my pack ~~with~~
the desk girls who speak no english. But the
ticket clerk did in the blue room I was directed
~~to at the station~~ and wrote it too on the back
of my Regency breakfast ticket: "today morning
nine." So an express to Datong K44 at 9:16

window
out at
head height
for light

entrance

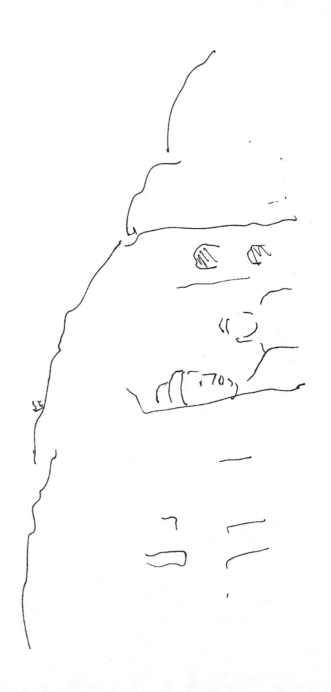

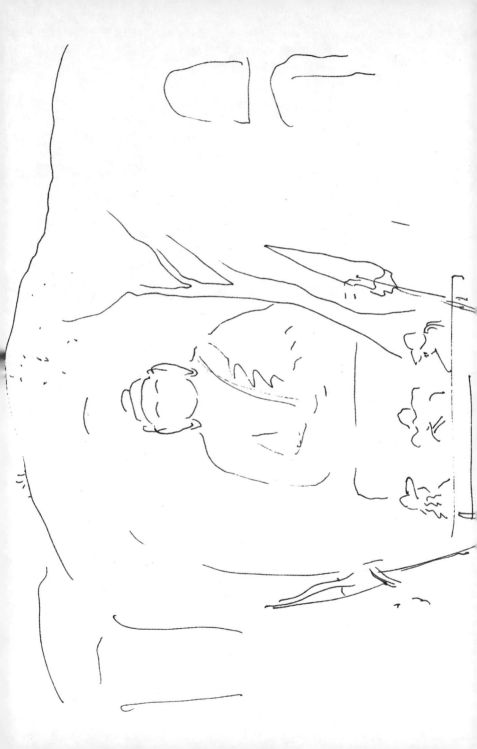

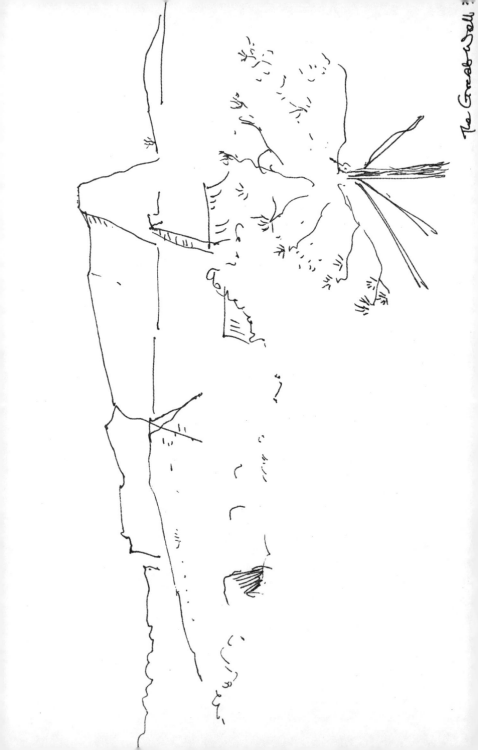

The Great Stell

5am Datong

Krisz roha! Krisz roha! (Thinking of yesterday, the best day of the trip: how I made it just in time to the caves, by way of the colliery, that little yellow battery operated ten seater trolley and the little boy squinting at me through the back of his seat and the girl turning her head to stare when she thought I wasn't looking, then even when she knew I was. Awoke since three: can't miss this train. Nodcean out cd easily slip back into sleep. So sitting naked. a little chilled

— so slip on my black shirt and pull the duvet cover (always have to remove the quilt — Beijing Shanghai Xian Hohot) over my legs, back against the varnished redbrown, well chestnut bedhead, a clothes post beside me in the corner, antlered in the Chinese dragon style with balls and knobs, all wood furniture heavily red lacquered, or black metal hard double bed. dismal flats outside the window, pottery vase gilded in the other corner, hotwater register pipes, mammoth TV

more heating pipes, newer white gloss on the
opposite wall, a pedestal fan clunky — unlike
our Made in China pedestal fan! — in that corner
beyond the other double bed where my things
lie spread

Thermos
in
basin

back
pack

& cucumbers

trusty
Bata
sandals

double
Boubed

Two litre water bottle not my shower after all! Water had been turned on when I got back from the caves. And now I find hot water in the big red thermos and have, unimagined luxury, a hot shave. At Maqur Vihar flat then, not the pits as judged from the slummy staircase, the rough sandy back lane where even the unlevel paving breaks down. But the power poles and wiring heavy duty (and the wiring not crazy) because this is China and they don't have power failures. Shuang remembers just a few from her Beijing childhood. Victorian plumbing though, the sewage pipes exposed in the bathroom and the S bend hangs over your head from the upstairs flat. Squat toilet has a little shield at the front end where the water is and a dip in the back: punch button flush from an exposed pipe. All the exposed pipes are slipper racks. And you shower over the toilet bowl, missteps unforgiven.

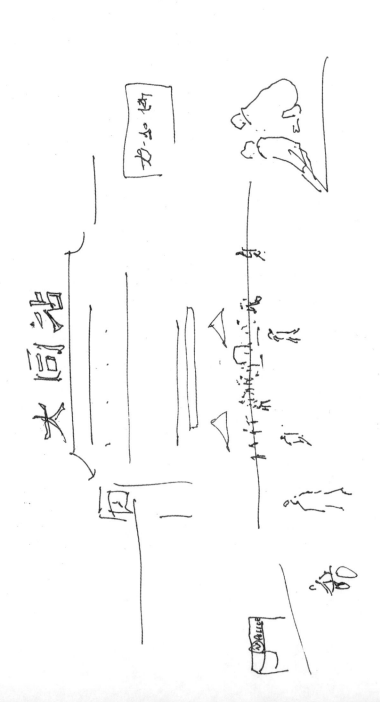

2.30   on the fast train K616 to Beijingxi

The guard salutes the train, holds his salute. Vineyards cover this stretch 2hrs out of Beijing, the same yellow clayey soil, dry and weathered into occasional ravines, that occurs in the Shanxis. A lake, a man fishing, an orchard of some kind of prunus. More of those mounds that are their cemeteries with the occasional granite tablet upright and also in the north half ring of concrete with the soil heaped up conically and a capstone

Loess? That painted the race over millennia?

Wide paved spaces are easy to keep clean — with an army of cleaners. Platform 1 this morning spotless and too the wide square in front of the railway station — a playground at night the lane by my apartment block at night was paved after all, but gritty and littered

Tunnels now, and towering crags stratified like puff pastry this carriage half empty, the first I've struck: nice and quiet and cool

奥发丁

Stainless steel
bin on Platform 1

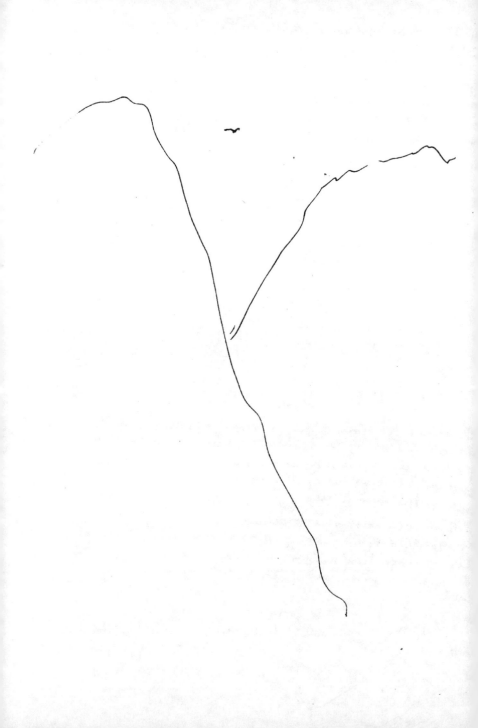

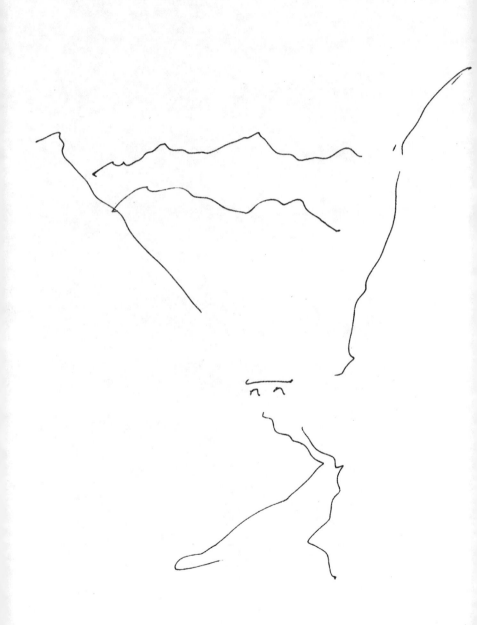

Afterword

In the summer of 2010 I went to China with a group of
Indian writers. I carried no camera, just a blank sketchbook. I'd had months to pack, but as always at the end
there was a scramble, and on the bus from the airport in
Beijing I found I'd left my sketch pen behind.

The first glimpse of a country is a profound mystery,
verging on sacrament. Nothing in the days or weeks to
follow can match those first raw moments. Everything is
new-born and tingling, and the longer you have lived with
the idea of that country the keener your exhilaration in
the airport bus. You could be on a far planet. Your spirit

goes questing out the window and it's some while before you remember you must take all this down. You pull out your sketchbook and pat your pockets, every pocket twice, for your sketch pen. There begins a frenzied, doomed scrabbling in your pack. Precious moments are lost cursing as the truth dawns on you. God and every angel will forgive you, but they won't deliver up your sketch pen, snug in a pigeonhole of the mapmaker's desk back in Dehra Dun. In despair you snatch up the blue writing pen.

Blue is not a colour I favour in inks. Blue is sky, and sea perhaps, not land. It must have been a standby, that pen, carried simply to eke out my store of black. With the greatest reluctance I filled the first few pages, a hobble at my elbow just when everything was flashing past, demanding shorthand. I may even have wished for a camera then. But a camera, I've always felt, is a toy. Even as a tool it has its limitations: you don't get a hold on a thing, you skim its surfaces. When you sketch, if the time is right, the essence of a thing passes into you. You draw closer to it and it to you; in a strange fleeting way you claim it because you've dwelt on it, or in it, and it claims you. You certainly grasp it the better, and hold the moment of that encounter.

Travelling one time as a younger man from the Yukon to the Yucatan I did carry a camera, an old single-lens reflex, but it's my sketchbook of that journey I cherish, not the woeful and now mouldering stash of Kodachrome transparencies.

Also, I've found when travelling, a sketchbook makes you friends, a camera enemies.

At the hotel of the Wo Fo Si, the Reclining Buddha, where we were housed next door to the botanical gardens, no black pens were to be had either, and it was a day or two before we went in to Beijing and any kind of shop. I cadged a black gel pen and began to draw. I have no illusions about my drawing, which I've always seen as the work of an amateur, the Sunday painter on Monday, a scribbler, a note-taker. The present book simply preserves those notes.

It's a commonplace book, a pillow book, or satchel book, that folio in which the first Francis Bacon, renaissance man, entered with diligence rather than prophetic fury, the things that struck him during the course of a day. So I sat in the conference room of the hotel with my fellow countrymen, facing the China side across a shining table broad as the Yangtze, and twiddled the borrowed gel pen, listening now to the flow of discourse, now to the distracting stream of phenomena, tracing the eddies at that vortex where the two met in the pendant on Zhai Yongming's necklace.

In Beijing were string recitals—the lute master Li Xiangting, playing the guqin, and our own Bahauddin Dagar on the rudra veena—readings at Tsinghua University, talks, discussions, sights to see, garden walks, a video screening of the new work of Kabir Mohanty. After Beijing we were treated to Shanghai, and then the conference was done.

The programme over, I stayed on. I had thought to stay back if my ticket could be changed, but had made no travel plans, had no bookings, much less an itinerary. One night under the ginkgos of the hotel courtyard I sat with Li Tuo, doyen of the China side, and Ashis Nandy, our own philosopher, talking of Hannibal the Carthaginian. Presently talk turned to the Terracotta Warriors and then to travel. I asked Li Tuo's advice and laid some plans, at least for my outward journey from Beijing. Go to Xian, he said, and then decide which way to turn.

On the last day Ouyang Jianghe, poet-militant, calligraphist and sorcerer, contrived to change my ticket. At what cost he was almost moved to say, but bit his tongue. I was free to stay. And so, waving goodbye to my friends at the airport, I returned to Beijing, bestowed the nursery ginkgos a millionaire had gifted me on our interpreter, Shuang Shen, and boarded the overnight train to Xian.

Xian is the old imperial capital of China, an inland St Petersburg. Travelling from Beijing, you might be going from Calcutta to Delhi, only you do it in fewer hours and on a sleek train. On arrival I put the luxury of the soft sleeper behind me and caught a city bus to the old town. The cheap hotels, I'd heard, were clustered by the ancient Hui mosque. I stood all the way hugging my rucksack, amazed that I should be on a Chinese bus going to the Hui quarter. I took the first room I was shown, basic but spacious and scrubbed clean, astonished at the price, a tenth of what everyone had predicted. I'd lucked into a 'Chinese' hotel; foreigners and well-off Chinese stop elsewhere. The sheets were spotless, the towel frayed but fresh. I threw open the window, inhaled deeply, and found myself above a bakery. I did a wild jig in the middle of the wooden floor. Sobering up I did a few simple sums, then wasted precious moments cursing. Had I known I could sleep at this price I'd have asked for twice as long on my ticket! God and his angels would have frowned now. I put away childishness and ran out into China.

I got lost straight away. Days later I discovered my window overlooked not just a bakery but the courtyard of the great mosque. But that first day I wandered the streets, fingering fallen leaves, rubbing the granite of benches, sniffing the air. Entranced by a Sunday pavement market, I stared like a peasant at mounds of steaming sheep's trotters, fruit stalls stacked with persimmons and walnuts, figs, wrinkled dates and lichis. I peered in at restaurant windows, tempted, but only theoretically; reflected in the glass I saw our twelve days of feasting, banquets thrown in the heroic Chinese style, sometimes two on the same day, when I gorged in company that I might starve twelve days on my own. Fate had rewarded me, now I would live narrow to travel wide.

What was I looking for? I couldn't have said, but it wasn't novelty. Pushed, I might hazard that I stayed on in search of a China I knew without ever having been there. Or half knew. Wherever I've been in my travels I've gravitated towards my own kind. Not my countrymen—those I'm inclined to avoid abroad. I mean my own level among the locals. A poor man abroad notices the poor, a rich man compares the local rich. I had no interest in meeting a peasant or a billionaire, not even in seeing how they lived; such encounters might interest a television reporter or somebody writing up China, hungry for the whole spectrum. My own inclination was quite the opposite. I think I was looking for a town that answered to my hometown Dehra Dun, and a man who might look like me.

What might we have in common? I think that was what interested me. The differences are countless; the sketch pen laps them up. But what of the commonalities? For only there could I judge fair. I had taken China at its word as a youth. America, Russia, Mexico, Italy, one by one they jilt you. So I looked out for and latched on to certain faces and streets, birds and trees. You don't travel to confirm your prejudices, but equally you hope to get past the facade of the 'classic'. A bridge will look so perfectly 'Chinese' it can only belong in a book. Of course you sketch it, but try as you might you can't trust its given age or even its purpose; it's a mythic bridge—even to the Chinese—part of the storied world, of dynasties, of revolutions, of restoration. But where is the world you recognize, the man who could be you? There, perhaps, you would be qualified to decide.

Sign language, goodwill and plain luck saw me through from day to day, but the futility of my search was guaranteed from the start. A few moments of sober thought should have convinced me that my other was unreachable, my hometown one of a kind. Datong, a town that in some ways qualified to be a pair to Dehra Dun, like the twin atom at the opposite end of the universe, showed me how unreasonable was my quest. If nothing else my ignorance of the Chinese language would have hamstrung me. It's not that opposite numbers don't exist, but how do you prove them? I still believe that a person exactly like me, neither rich nor poor, muddling along, exists out there (the way you see doubles of people you know in far countries) and that I would learn more about China from him than from fifty peasants. I also know the odds against meeting him are unbeatable. You meet what you meet and make of it what you will. My best bet was a pen allowed to travel a little ahead of me, taking dictation from chance.

A tourist moves trustingly through light and air and buildings, dodging bicycles and colliding with strangers, and returns to sort through his preconceptions. From childhood on, my China—as if I spoke of porcelain!—was pictorial, a willow-pattern plate of images: the moon in a

lake with a man in a boat, quirks in roof and hat and sail—
a way of loading the watercolour brush. In real life it was
a friend's Swan fountain pen at school, engineered as we
somehow couldn't in India; a character in steam over a
winter bowl of noodles; a graphic novel that told a story
of heroic resistance to the invading Japanese, ant-like
black-uniformed soldiers picked out in terrifying silhou-
ette on the crest of a hill. How could you, at eleven, not
detest the invader, how could you not love the heroine? I
can still see those black-and-white line drawings, each
frame as beautifully engraved as the Swan fountain pen
cap, can still feel floppy heft of that landscape format
comic book. It appeared mysteriously in our house just at
the time of our war with China, and I recall my mother
worried that I might appear to be consorting with the
enemy. After that there was only Mao and the little red
book. Of the famines I knew nothing.

So we build our pictures of foreign lands, our com-
posite globe. A curious (and partly spurious) sense of
brotherhood, of discovered kinship seems to knit Asiatics
together, even those from societies so disparate as China
and India. It is perhaps simply a shared otherness to the
West, although with every Chinese technological triumph

the burden of that otherness falls more heavily on India. But every eager unready arrival on the airport bus comes armed with a foreknowledge that begs to be undone. And the honest recording of his impressions is one way out of the bind. Balsam poplar, erect, sweet-scented, shimmering, a tree to adore, greets him first thing on the airport free-way. Suddenly, without warning, another deity—the Himalayan deodar! By the time he is in town, with electric rickshaws whizzing by in the slow lane and glass and steel towering above, a rift in him has begun to heal. All his life he's swung between the Europe of his head and the India of his heart. Anybody who's spent nights in that hammock will know the discontents of such a division; the thought that a nation just might be built—is here *being* built—to straddle ancient and modern in a new way is a kind of comfort.

For the Chinese we are, I suspect, a little quaint. It doesn't help that for centuries we were an inspiration in matters other-worldly, engineering as they somehow couldn't. Today we are a competitor who has fallen behind in the economic race. I felt at times a little like the Japanese visitor to Europe a hundred years ago, envious, impatient to learn, tempted to spy. My special field needed no hidden camera; I could sit outside a police station with my sketchbook and go about my business. What threat could I possibly be?

Of course in between sketches you're moved to record events, things spoken, a satisfying meal. Handwriting had got me into trouble once, outside an army installation in Egypt, detained for hours while my minuscule Roman script was deciphered. But that was forty years ago. Here I wrote in peace. Any kind of record made with the hand is already in the realm of the archaic; today's spy takes digital notes. Only a harmless antiquarian would bother with a pen. So the sketchbook is equally a diary, if a dull one. No conquests, few scrapes. Usually I left a blank page between sketches; then when I appeared to be running out of space, I went back to such pages and used them to compile lists. They could be anything. A menu (for our daughter who, from the time she was little, demanded a detailed account of any meal she was going to miss), an anti-shopping list, useful words in Mandarin, local flora. The trees of China were a pleasure ever since I found the purple bauhinia of Hong Kong flowering at precisely the same time as the one at our gate. Only the birds disappointed, falling silent, hiding their plain faces, burrowing deeper into the trees. No fantail to flit right up to you and perch on your shoulder, filling your ear with chit-chat.

Sketching, you're aware that you're on air, live. A slip of the pen is there for good; there's no Delete. This facsimile edition was never intended, and it is a merciless master. Certain pages make me cringe, but there they are. It is also a good moderator: you can't overegg the pudding. A sketch, even when it fails, has a point; a botched page tells you something. Don't pass this way again, don't sit too long; go lightly. Kiss, don't tell. But do you learn? Again and again you blot your copy-book. But little by little you surrender to the newness. Leafing through now, I can watch that happening. Cookies on a plate, a cellphone tower, every familiar thing is recast under this new sky. Threshold, roof tile, kettle, clothes-horse, ladle, chair— all known forms intrigue and delight, shaped to please another god. Alert to difference, you sift millennia. A city wall, a gate, stone roads deeply rutted by centuries of cart wheels, the antique has its own appeal, but so does a stainless-steel dustbin.

Axioms in philosophy must be proved *upon the pulse*, Keats muses in a letter I took to heart long ago. Only the sensorium does not lie; what we smell, taste, touch is to trust, before logic. Revisionist historians teach us this without meaning to: tomorrow all their labours will be overturned. The things you experience are experienced fresh each time. In the quiet lane just inside the Pingyao city wall, four girls fresh from Wuhan corral me with their bicycles and watch me sketch. I'm copying a pattern of brick lace above a gate I mean to take back and use. I tell them I'm a bricklayer, which is not a lie. They dismount and gather around to practise their English. All except one have Western names, or perhaps nicknames; the exception is the quiet one. We talk of China, of India. Which of us, their leader asks suddenly, tiring of geography, is the most beautiful? It's a hard decision for a susceptible man, but they stand there under their eyelashes, waiting. I shut my eyes, turn slowly all the way round, and—peeping to make sure—lay a finger on Shi Jiao. They burst out laughing at the pantomime. Now we can talk freely. I put down my sketchbook and for ten minutes we simply gas. When they're gone, waving madly, a woman of my age approaches along the same lane. I greet her with a smile as wide as the one the girls left me. She returns a stony stare and passes on.

I didn't mean to go to Pingyao. At Xian railway station I'd stood in a queue for a ticket to Yulin, a town on the Great Wall. It looked like the kind of place no one would want to go to, like Sisal, that forgotten port at the bottom of Mexico. But when I got to the ticket window I was told there was no train. Thrown, I recast the dice. Pingyao, city of Ming courtyards, rose up. Beyond lay Inner Mongolia! And I would just have time for Datong on the way back to Beijing. But the nearest I got to Mongol grasslands was a conservatory lawn. Hohhot, capital of Inner Mongolia, is a Han city now, the balance of population tipped, like that of Tibet, by continued immigration. It was as dull as New Delhi, bland as Canberra. I turned to Datong, famous for its Buddha caves, with relief.

In Datong I struck at last an ordinary Chinese flat. Its owner was a woman standing under a red umbrella at the railway station; she wrote down a price—of the room, I hoped—and we turned and walked down the street. The public works of Datong, grand to grandiose, abolished any comparison I might hope to make with my home town; the apartment made me grateful for our house in Dehra Dun. One of the last sketches I made in China was of its bathroom, and for that I turned to an earlier blank page, opposite the sketch I'd made of the bathroom in the millionaire's suite in Shanghai, mine for two nights while he was away. On my way to the Buddha caves I passed through the workers' township at Datong's collieries and was again grateful. I bowed before the transplanted Buddha, serene these two thousand years. Returning, I caught a glimpse of the Great Wall, an earthen cairn, but of the dwellers of my apartment, apparently hastily evacuated for the night, I saw nothing at all. Just their rubber bathroom slippers, tucked in a row behind an exposed water pipe, staring at me like owls on a wire.

Back in Beijing, Shuang Shen, inspired interpreter, was waiting anxiously, afraid I might have slipped through a fault, gone missing in her country. With just a few hours to my flight she took me shopping, helped me pack my ginkgos. Her flat in the Drum and Gong hutong was furnished just as ours at home; her bookshelves, her kitchen, her very towel-rail approximated mine. Clearly I'd been looking in the wrong place for my twin, and at last on the metro to the airport the penny dropped. My China double was a woman!

At the Xian Sunday market I'd bought a kilo of lichis. That very week, the first week of June, was the height of our own lichi season at home, and I would miss it. Lichis were brought to India from China about the time tea was, and cultivated across the north. I was just thinking the same might be done for the ginkgo when the man at Delhi airport ushered me aside to the botanical office. My heart sank. But it was past midnight and there was a lock on the door. The man smiled defeat and waved me through the Green Channel.

My first concern on returning home was to plant this treasure. The summer was hot and cripplingly dry, but the rains were due and waterlogging might hurt the plants too. I must pick my spot with care—two different spots, to play it safe. Towards the end of that monsoon one of the ginkgos appeared to sicken. The leaves turned black and fell off and I feared it was about to rot and die. It didn't, but there was a fortnight in there when I felt life was not worth living. Today the convalescent is still in search of suitable ground, dug up again and again and transplanted, while its mate prospers, twice as big, in its first bed. They are my living links with China.

I brought back something else: a pagoda. A whole pagoda, in my head. The Small Wild Goose Pagoda. Across the miles the original in Xian, built to honour the seventh-century dharma master Du Shun, seeded the tower I built when I got home. It seeded too the *book* of the building of that tower. *The Small Wild Goose Pagoda* tells the story of our plot of land in Dehra Dun, a natural and social history of 433 square yards of India. The story also of the men who helped me build, alongside the house my father built, a habitable tower. A modernist tower that unites two contradictory Chinese architectural tropes: the hatted pagoda and the open sky-well, that shaft at the heart of a building that lets in air and light. In the book I honoured mistri, mazdoor and mali—mason, labourer and gardener, three men who taught me their craft—as well as my family. Filial piety certainly, but also a workbook, a manual. A book of life.

It's not finished of course, the pagoda. It'll see me out. The beauty of it can still catch me unawares, the detailing is a source of continuing pleasure, and the loving expense of spirit it entails will solace my old age. There is still an iron door to paint, a staircase to put in. Just the other day I found three old teak beams at the kabaris—the scrapsellers—that will make the treads. A mural too awaits, in blue, and a cutout tin frieze of the animals you find on ornamented roof ridges in China that will surround the glass chimney at the sky-well. The rescued mapmaker's desk below, lit by falls of natural light, never got a coat of varnish.

Some days though I feel it's time to sign a quietus, and I look for a ceremony or a gesture that will put a seal on the proceedings. Surely the time has come to sit back and enjoy my ivory, yet lustrous white, tower? Perhaps next year, when it's whispered we are to return to China, I'll bring back a wind chime from some remote province and instal it above the glass chimney. Then every time the house breathes news will come from Xanadu.

And I'll put my feet up on the mapmaker's desk, and do nothing.